Endorsements for *What to Say and How to Say It:*

The first time I've seen this topic so sharply defined with real solutions to everyday difficult workplace issues. It offers examples that *everyone* in the organization can use immediately.

What to Say and How to Say It is like having your own personal coach guiding you through difficult relationships daily. If you like the idea of having your own coach, get this book and keep it by your side.

In our age-diverse workplace of conflicting work ethics, incongruent values, and contrasting styles, this book offers fresh examples that can be applied to daily situations immediately.

A quick clear read—the seventy-two tips are for *everyone*. These examples can be applied personally, professionally, and as citizens in our communities. The examples and solutions will help liberate ourselves from interactions that create pain.

Roz Jeffries, Author, *101 Recognition Secrets*
PEG, Inc.: Developing People, Ideas and Organizations

That folk want to communicate is obvious ... that folk struggle with their personal communication is the sad dilemma of our age. Bill and Carolyn Hines fully rectify that in this splendid book! They raise our respect and knowledge of others to new heights, including new motivation toward giving our best efforts in our relationships. The wisdom they offer both fills and transcends the workplace, spilling over into other spaces of our lives!

Rev. Dr. Paige Lanier Chargois
Associate Professor, Richmond Virginia Seminary
Author, Retired Pastor

The courage it takes to appropriately communicate is *daunting* indeed! Carolyn and Bill Hines—with great skill and sensitivity—eliminate most of the risk and leave their readers with understanding and skill to address many situations, whether at work or in other circumstances.

What to Say and How to Say It serves as a perfect desk reference, training manual, gift book—a must-have for anyone who wishes to improve their communication skills.

Dr. Deloris Saunders, Past President
National Association of Black School Educators
Chief of Professional Development,
Department of Defense

Bill and Carolyn Hines rank among the best of trainers, consultants, and executive coaches who inspire us and guide us in promoting healthier relationships! In *What to Say and How to Say It*, they provide insightful and practical skills through entertaining and helpful, specific words to use in making relationships more successful! Every single one of us needs help from time to time in navigating courageous conversations. Search no longer! This much-needed resource is now in your hands.

Lori Hobson
Author, *Momma's Sayings*

What to Say
and How to Say It

72 Courageous Conversations for the Workplace

Emotional Intelligence Skills
How-Tos for Entering, Engaging, and Exiting Necessary Dialogue

WILLIAM and CAROLYN HINES

iUniverse, Inc.
New York   Bloomington

What to Say and How to Say It
72 Courageous Conversations for the Workplace

iUniverse books may be ordered through booksellers or by contacting:

iUniverse
1663 Liberty Drive
Bloomington, IN 47403
www.iuniverse.com
1-800-Authors (1-800-288-4677)

ISBN: 978-1-4502-1267-0 (sc)
ISBN: 978-1-4502-1268-7 (ebk)

Printed in the United States of America

iUniverse rev. date: 03/30/2010

For our children, Michael Hines, Thomas Bullock, and Kimberly Hines Bullock; our grandchildren, Symone and Olyvia Bullock; and the many participants in our training sessions who encouraged us to write down "real words" to use for courageous conversations.

See what you have—the past;

See what you want—the present;

See what can be—the future!

—from *Living Successfully with Screwed-Up People*
by Elizabeth Brown

Contents

Foreword

We live in a world where communication abounds. We have iPods, iPhones, PCs, BlackBerrys, you name it. We "IM" each other and communicate through Facebook, LinkedIn, and Twitter. And yet, many of us fail to have the meaningful face-to-face conversations that are essential to building relationships and solving difficult workplace issues. It's key that we have these conversations, as communication is the glue that cements relationships and holds successful organizations together.

The great sales communicator Earle Nightingale once said that "the effectiveness of one's life is determined by the effectiveness of one's communicative skills." People are misled, deals are not made, and thoughts are never delivered because people fail to communicate courageously and openly with others.

With this book, Carolyn and William Hines provide useful information on what to say, how to say it, and when to say it—or better yet, what not to say at all. They help you examine your answers to some of the following questions:

- Have you often thought of exactly what you wanted to say to someone … the next day or even weeks later?
- Have you stood by and said nothing while observing someone being treated unfairly or badly?
- Have you been treated disrespectfully and did not know how to respond?
- Have you wanted to address the behavior of a friend, family member, neighbor, colleague, manager, or subordinate and did not know how to phrase your remarks?
- Can you say no to requests and situations without feeling guilty?
- Are you comfortable asking for what you want and deserve?
- Are you comfortable asking for help, offering help, and saying, "I don't know?"
- Can you state your position, offer suggestions, and ask for clarification in clear, assertive language?
- Are you nervous when interacting with "higher-ups"?
- How do you receive and respond to criticism?

- Are you uncomfortable when you have to deal with a very sensitive situation and feel you don't have the courage to do it?

All of us struggle at times with finding the right words to say to an employee, a friend, a spouse, or a neighbor. We tend to be timid and hide our true feelings because we are not sure how to respond. *What to Say and How to Say It* provides us with a guide or road map on how to handle difficult situations and do so in a most professional manner.

What to Say and How to Say It is loaded with priceless information and skills that have been espoused by the Hineses over the years. There is nothing magical about these teachings, as they are anchored in timeless principles and common sense. Take for instance Skill #11, which simply states, "Remember that you have two ears and one mouth, so spend twice as much time listening as you do talking." It's a proven fact that the best communicators are not the best talkers; they are the best listeners.

This book is written for those of you who want to become better communicators and more comfortable interacting with others. It is for those who want to walk away from every conversation knowing that they have communicated their message in a most professional, courageous, courteous, and meaningful manner.

Analyze one skill a week for a year, think about it, and put it into practice. If you commit to doing this, I can assure you that you will become a better communicator, one who is respected by those you talk with. Like anything in life, it will take hard work, but it will be well worth the time you invest.

Hugh Gouldthorpe
Author of *I've Always Looked Up to Giraffes:*
Discover Why Some People and Organizations
Stand Head and Shoulders Above the Crowd
and Inspire Others to Reach New Heights
Senior Vice President,
Quality and Communications
Owens and Minor

Preface

The Need for This Book

Over the past decade, tension in the workplace has been the focus of news coverage, books, and articles. There has been an increase in grievances and arbitrations based on undue emotional distress, along with a rise in stress-related complaints. More and more of our clients are requesting specific services to address conflict management and its relationship to organizational development. More and more articles and books are being published on the benefits of emotional-intelligence skill building and its relationship to stress management and quality of life. The time is right for a book that ties all of these elements together.

Acknowledgments

We give special thanks to our daughter, Kim Hines Bullock, and our associates, Herb Mclure and Joyce Boisson, for their early editing of this manuscript; to our son, Michael, for his unwavering support; to our editorial consultant, Cathy Raymond at iUniverse, for her meticulous and patient guidance; and to our parents, George and Melva Walker and William and Carolyn Hines. They are truly the "wind beneath our wings."

Introduction

For more than twenty years, management consultants and certified mediators William and Carolyn Hines have facilitated team building, executive coaching, conflict management, leadership, and emotional-intelligence skill training and education for hundreds of client groups across the public and private sectors. They have experienced firsthand the results of significantly improved working relationships as a result of participants learning and practicing courageous conversations.

What is it about straight talk, communicating directly, and engaging conflict that makes us so nervous? Do we believe that avoiding issues, problems, and concerns helps us to be accepted by others? And even when compliments and thank-yous are extended, they are oftentimes discounted:

"Margaret, what a terrific job you did on that presentation!"
"I was just doing my job."

"Jake, what a lovely tie"
"You mean this old thing?"

And what about situations that produce recurring hurt, confusion, loss of confidence, frustration, and stress leading to illness, violence, and an increase in identified rages: road rage, air rage, work rage, school rage?

In organizations, how often have you seen a non-performing employee ignored or relocated rather than dealt with directly and in a manner helpful to the employee and the organization? Or watched a relationship erode or a family dissolved because of conflict avoidance? More often than not, we find ourselves nervous about, and therefore avoiding, face-to-face dialogue with someone whose behavior we find less than positive. How do we normally deal with confrontation? Could it be through one of these avoidance techniques?

- Talking about or complaining about the person to other people
- Sending an anonymous letter
- "Dropping" hints
- Deliberate nonverbals (eye-rolling, sighing, hand gestures)
- Tattling on the other person to another person in a perceived authoritative role
- Praying for a miracle—that the person leaves, gets sick, or dies
- Avoiding the person altogether and staying stuck in negative emotions

- Staying stuck in the past and becoming a prisoner of your past
- Speaking directly with the person and asking for the behaviors you want to receive or need from others

What to Say and How to Say It—based on the compelling research supporting emotional intelligence and the work of Daniel Goleman, author of *Working With Emotional Intelligence* and *Social Intelligence*—gives specific prompts or language helpful for entering, engaging in, and exiting courageous conversations. Courageous conversations are those discussions we all need to have, oftentimes with people we care about, don't care about, or need to care about. These are the conversations that will help us make it through difficult times, get over hurdles that are blocking relationship-building, and improve living and working conditions for everyone involved. Skills in courageous conversations help to build emotional intelligence. And you also have the opportunity to model the way for others.

Learning how to have these conversations can involve years of training, and this skill is the stock in trade for a number of professions. We don't pretend to be able to convey all that information in this little book, and we aren't going to try to make you into a skilled counselor or therapist. But we know that everyone sometimes needs a way to get a conversation started and a way to get to the heart of an issue effectively, and that's what we're trying to help you with. This is written mainly for people in work settings: supervisors and managers who need to address workplace issues. It can also be helpful to employees at all levels who need help or information from their supervisors, managers, or colleagues. Also, these are conversations we need to have outside the workplace. We have occasionally pointed out how the same courageous-conversation guidelines can help in family and other settings.

Learning and practicing courageous conversations helps to build skill in emotional intelligence, which Daniel Goleman defined in his 2006 book, *Working with Emotional Intelligence*, as "the capacity for recognizing our own feelings and those of others, for motivating ourselves, and for managing emotions well in ourselves and in our relationships."

We are humans and social by nature, thus impacted by relationships. What others do affects our emotions, and those emotions affect our health and well-being, especially in the presence of high levels of stress. Emotional intelligence helps you promote collaborative behavior by:

- Directing behavior toward positive outcomes in building caring relationships
- Understanding that emotionally healthy communication combines choice words and caring actions
- Communicating openly through helpful and respectful language
- Accurately understanding and stating needs
- Displaying predictable and flexible behavior

- Avoiding threats, bluffs, and intimidation
- Using logical and innovative approaches to presenting views, especially for problem-solving
- Avoiding stereotyping, jumping to conclusions, or making assumptions; valuing diversity
- Determining what is possible or impossible in relationships
- Accepting responsibility for your half of every relationship you are in and doing 100 percent of your half to impact healthy relationships
- Seeing yourself as others see you and applying that feedback to self-management
- Recognizing what is causing tension and that emotionally secure relationships involve compromise and negotiation
- Being willing to change first because you know that what you do and how you react to others is your responsibility
- Controlling your own actions and reactions by understanding that behavior patterns and habits are not etched in stone
- Knowing that if you want a different outcome, your thoughts and behaviors must change
- Approaching relationship difficulties as opportunities to improve
- Keeping "you should" from burdening interactions

Chapter 1

Skills for Developing the "Courageous Conversation" Mind-Set

People must believe in each other, and feel that it can be done and must be done; in that way they are enormously strong. We must keep up each other's courage.
—*Vincent Van Gogh*

Before revving up our courage to engage someone important to us (or not so important) in a courageous conversation, our minds need to be disciplined toward the outcomes we want or need. We refer to these mind-sets as *guiding* or *mental principles* that help to maintain focus. Let's discuss a few guiding principles for courageous conversations. Each of these principles represents a belief system that becomes a skill base. Believe that you can use these principles in the situations you encounter. This belief system allows you to apply several of our suggestions for what to say, when to say it, and how to say it.

Skill #1: Strengthen your emotional mind-set by touching others with your words (beginning with the ending you have in mind). Here are courageous thoughts—requiring strength of brain and emotion— that lead to courageous conversations and help you produce positive outcomes. Remember that you feel tension or pressure in a relationship because you care. When responding to others, project positive energy and outcomes.

"Darla, I will have an answer for you by _____."

"Dan, count on me to _____. This is what I'm willing to do."

"David, I will be happy to support you on _____. I want to _____."

"Danita, I feel certain we will do better on _____."

"Devon, please know how much I care, because I know the two of us can make this agreement work."

"Damien, let's laugh about this miscommunication and start over."

Refuse to be a victim and refuse to be helpless. Make clear statements. Cohesion and positive outcomes for working relationships require careful choices in words that you use in communicating with others. (Remember that anger can be both your ally and your enemy.)

"Ellie, I feel like a victim, and here's how."

"Ed, right now I am feeling pretty helpless, and here's how."

"Esther, I refuse to be set up on this issue. Let's get the parties involved right now."

Deliver at least three compliments a day. Get in the habit of making uplifting comments to others, especially those you may find it difficult to deal with.

"Mattie, it's good seeing you today."

"Malik, what a happy tie!"

"Marsha, thanks for getting right back to me."

Be relentless in searching for and making positive comments to others. Ask for what you want. People cannot read your mind.

"Jake, what two things need to happen differently for you to get to work on time?"

"Jody, please tell me one thing I can trust you to do to make this suggestion work."

"Jimmy, I love it when you participate in the staff meeting."

Make being pleasant, caring, and helpful a priority. Remember that pleasantness, caring, and helpfulness are all *skills.*

"Rita, let's agree on one thing we can do to help Patsy with this project."

"Randy, we are a strong unit, and we can do this. Let's start planning right now!"

"Rachel, here's what I am going to do to help you. Would you please accept my help?"

Listen for opportunities and prompt others to "opportunity thinking."

"Ann, I sense an opportunity here instead of an obstacle. Here's how."

"Alex, let's concentrate on one way we can make this work."

"Al, I sense frustration. What do you suggest we do next?"

Credit your success to helpful relationships.

"I could not have achieved this recognition without the direct support of Alice and Fred. They are the best. They made this honor possible, and I am grateful for

how they keep me on task and bring a warm spirit to our work team."

"Jann, you deserve credit for _____."

"Jeffers, I am lost with you and your _____."

"Jonnie, thank you for being my guardian angel."

Identify and eliminate clutter in your personal space and in your relationships. Be a model of orderliness and calmness. Clear away unnecessary paper and knickknacks. Keep your work area neat, welcoming, and easily accessible to others. Limit contact with people who are truly toxic and determined to stay that way. Recognize that your "hot buttons" are alarms to unresolved issues. Call people on "awfulizing" and "stinking thinking" (terms created by noted psychologist Dr. Albert Ellis).

"Pete, please say something positive—I know you can!"

"Paula, hearing you make mean statements about Mike makes me nervous about what you say about me when I am not present."

"Pamela, please stop finding fault and make just one positive suggestion, please."

Accept responsibility and accountability.

"Barbara, I will take responsibility for _____."

*"Ben, I will take the lead on _____ and be fully
accountable for _____."*

*"Brad, let me sit with you for a few minutes and
make a to-do list."*

Practice good listening habits. Double-check that you
have heard what someone is saying before you start
talking. Remember the two-to-one rule: You have two
ears and one mouth. Spend twice as much time listening
as you do talking.

"George, I want to make sure I heard you correctly."

*"Gina, please go over that one more time. I want to
be sure I listened intently."*

*"Gigi, I am working on building my listening skills,
so call me on it when you think I need to be more
attentive."*

Make changes gradually. Ask for and act on feedback.

*"Carl, here's how I am working on changing. [Identify
the specific behavior.] Would you periodically let me
know how I am doing?"*

"Casey, here's where I am struggling to change."

*"Craig, I desperately need to know if I have made
even just a little improvement."*

Promise only what you can deliver.

> *"Fred, I simply cannot deliver on that request."*

> *"Frances, here's exactly what you can depend on me to deliver."*

> *"Frank, I will let you know immediately when snags occur."*

Watch your biases. State them and ask for monitoring.

> *"Hank, I struggle with hearing what someone is saying when face piercings are so evident."*

> *"Heather, here's my bias about people who are chronically late."*

> *"Herb, I have a bias toward people from Virginia."*

Develop good delegation skills.

> *"Jill, here's the project I need you to take the lead on, and here's the flexibility you have."*

> *"Jake, I need to trust you to _____."*

> *"Joni, I am delegating this task to you, and here's why this task is important."*

Own and state your emotions.

> *"Kelly, emotionally, here's where I am on this issue."*

*"Ken, I feel _____ [one word]. And here's what
I need from you."*

"Kathy, I want _____."

Trust your team and build trust with people close to you.

*"Larry, as a member of my team, 'trust' to me means
_____."*

"Leann, I want to trust you to _____."

*"Lorna, as my roommate, your trust is dear to me,
and I hope mine is to you."*

Develop and maintain cooperative relationships. Use the
word "cooperative" often in your dialogue with others:

*"Nina, cooperation to me can be defined in three
ways: _____."*

"Nick, let me know how I can be more cooperative."

*"Nathan, please tell me one thing you will do to be
more cooperative in meeting the requirements of this
action plan."*

**Skill #2: Help others realize their goals and your goals
in a caring and helpful way.** Oftentimes, courageous
conversations involve something we'd rather not have to
discuss. The reasons we go ahead and have the conversations
are that we feel we owe it to ourselves, we owe it to our

organization, and we want to help the other person if we can. For example, you wouldn't normally tell someone you know they smelled bad unless you were trying to help them in some way. So try to remember that's what you're doing when you have these conversations, and ask yourself whether the words you choose will sound like you care and are trying to be helpful.

Skill #3: Use kind, helpful, caring, and loving words, because no one bristles at them. The words we choose make an enormous difference in our lives, not because they change our meaning but because they allow the other person to understand our meaning. Using kind words helps people listen because the words tend to "land on their ears and hearts" more receptively.

Skill #4: No matter what the other person is doing or saying, try to respond in the most kind, helpful, caring, and loving way you can. People often use a conversation to express anger, fear, frustration, sorrow, joy, or happiness. We always have choices about how to respond. Sometimes we try to underplay, minimize, empathize; sometimes we agree. Sometimes the other person's emotions, whatever they are, trigger an irritating or hostile reaction, and we try to minimize those feelings. But if we want to have a real, helpful conversation, we have to listen carefully and try to respond in a way that encourages other people to be their best and do their best.

Skill #5: Get to know your co-workers, friends, and other people in your life and what is important to them. This is a key to building trust. We often encounter people who have worked together for years—side by side, in some cases—who know almost nothing about each other. A powerful exercise people sometimes do in groups is a simple but rich self-introduction, where you tell each other where you grew up, what your family life was like, what you see as your important personal or professional accomplishments, something you got away with in high school or college, and a talent or interest you have that others may not know about. These are life experiences people could discuss any day over coffee or lunch, or occasionally at a staff meeting, but don't. When you do and thereby learn more about each other, you form a different kind of relationship and are much more likely to try to trust and support each other in a team setting. Oftentimes, even family members really don't know each other or what is important to each other. Work on relationship building before issues and tasks. Remember that you own half of every relationship that you are in. We teach people how to treat us because we are predictable. Most of our lives, we interact with folks who are also predictable. Learn to communicate to the predictability of others, especially when you have a good idea of how the other person is likely to respond. For example: "Mark, I know you are likely to say no to my requests. This time, I trust you to hear me out and please say yes."

Skill #6: Remember that people are rational from their point of view, no matter how weird they may seem to you. People are smart, and they don't usually set out to do stupid things. So no matter how odd a behavior looks to you, remember that it may make sense from the other person's point of view. Understanding that things may make more sense from another point of view is one aspect of connecting with other people. Showing your respect for others is essential to developing effective teamwork, no matter how different that other person may seem to you. If you are willing to try to see a situation the way the other person sees it, you can have courageous conversations. Otherwise, you're mostly lecturing.

Skill #7: No matter what someone else does, ask yourself, "Could that person's intent be beneficial?" One of the reasons we don't more often intervene when we see adults screaming at children or even hitting them is that we assume they mean well. It will help you in any conversation if you go into it with that same attitude in mind. People often—maybe even most of the time— don't think through what they say in advance and end up saying what they say poorly. For example, think about how an executive who just gave a speech would respond to someone who said, "I think your remark that employees need to work harder was callous and insensitive and just shows how out of touch you are." Now let's look at another approach to the same statement: "I love this organization and respect you for trying to get it to become even more effective. I am deeply concerned about your response that employees need to work harder. Please give me two or three examples that I can apply and share with my colleagues." Press for understanding without defensiveness. If you understand the other person's beneficial intent, your interactions will tend to go better. Practice responses for exploring beneficial intent.

> *"Amman, walk me through how you see what you just said working. I want to really understand how you see that as beneficial."*

> *"Alita, I had not considered what you just said in that light. Tell me more."*

> *"Andrew, now that viewpoint is certainly something new."*

> *"Avon, wow—I never would have seen that if you had not said _____."*

Skill #8: Pick your battles by monitoring your reactions and how you take things personally. Many battles are simply not worth picking. More often than not, when you take things personally, what the other person is saying is not really about you, but about what is going on with them. Vow, right now, to stop taking issue with what you perceive as personal affronts, and choose not to see an insult—especially when no insult was intended. Even when insults are intended, they can only land if you give them power. No one insults you without your permission.

Skill #9: Choose to see all criticism as useful information. This is a tough skill requiring intense discipline, because just the thought of criticism can make you uneasy and often defensive. Remember that, when you become defensive, you are rendered incapable of thinking clearly. The brain goes haywire—thus the need for discipline. In your mind, understand that criticism can be seen as feedback. The emotional mind-set you take into a conversation has a lot to do with what the conversation accomplishes. Rather than reacting defensively (taking criticism too personally) to statements you interpret as criticism, we suggest you do two things: first, make sure you understood clearly what the person intended to say, and second, respond to it as information, not criticism. Say to yourself, "How can I use this information to make me better, to make our relationship better?" Oftentimes, you can simply agree with or even welcome the criticism and ask for suggestions on how you can be better. When the other person is predictable in delivering criticism, brace yourself to respond with statements like:

> *"Kaitlin, I know how you like to criticize me. It's okay; I welcome what you have to say."*

> *"Kelvin, you are right. I could have done a better job on this report. I will have a rewrite on your desk by noon."*

"Kara, let's explore your criticism a little closer. What else would you like to add to what you just said about my _____."

Skill #10: Model the change you want to see in others. It usually seems inconvenient to change, and most often we would like the world to change so we don't have to. So parents will yell at children about watching less TV and doing more homework, but they won't turn off the TV and help the kids with the homework. Unfortunately, it's almost always true that nothing you want to change will change unless you change too. This often means you have to do something you'd rather not do, like turning off the TV and helping the kids, or having a courageous conversation. Consider the manager who comments on your coming to a meeting late when that manager is renowned for being late.

Skill #11: Remember that you have two ears and one mouth, so spend twice as much time listening as you do talking. Nothing else needs to be said about this critical skill.

Chapter 2

Planning Courageous Conversations

It takes as much energy to wish as it does to plan.
—*Eleanor Roosevelt*

Now let's talk about how to actually engage in a courageous conversation. How can we move from talking to ourselves about wanting to say something to someone about something that lingers in our thoughts to actually having that conversation? These skills are akin to other skills we want to learn. If we want to be better golfers, we have to practice, play, practice, play, practice, play. Unless it's something we do every day professionally, most of us aren't prepared to have courageous conversations off the cuff. We don't think of the right things to say quickly enough, and we don't usually listen carefully enough.

So we suggest you take a few minutes and think the conversation through.

Skill #12: Decide what issue you want to raise or resolve in the conversation, and compose a sentence or two that describes the issue clearly. Use no more than nine to eleven words, or you will tend to start whining. Describe the outcome you want to achieve as a result of the conversation.

> *"Frankie, I am hurting about _____. Here's what I desperately most want from you: _____."*

> *"Fields, here's the issue: _____. What's the first step you recommend to move from this point?"*

> *"Fallon, 'resolved' to me means _____. What exactly does 'resolved' mean to you?"*

Too often, we start a conversation because we are concerned or upset about something, without thinking through what we would like the result of the conversation to be. Unless you know what you want, you aren't very likely to get it. When you know what you want, compose a sentence you can say to the other party that will tell him or her exactly what the issue is and exactly what you want in eleven words or less.

Imagine the responses the other person may offer and think through how the discussion might go. Ask a person whose feedback you value to role-play the conversation with you. Most people with whom we interact are predictable. Remember the principles we have already touched on about predicting the behavior of others. You may be able to preempt the other person by saying what that person is likely to say before she says it: "Mady, I know that you are likely to say no to my request for training. Please hear me out because I desperately need you to say yes to my request."

Think through how you want the issue to be resolved and the actions you think are essential. Write all of your responses down so that you stay focused on the outcome you want or need. Make sure you have a clear outcome before you allow the conversation to end. You are responsible for expressing yourself as clearly as you can. Be able to state what you want and what you are willing to do to bring positive energy to the relationship. Ask for forgiveness for your half of the relationship that has not gone well, and ask for a fresh start.

Stating the Issue—An Important Review

When courageous conversations don't address an issue, it's usually because the issue was never clearly stated. Therefore, again, we suggest that you write out and rehearse your statement of the issue before you begin the conversation. Your statement needs to be specific about when, where, what, and who.

"Fannie, yesterday you came to work wearing a tight see-through blouse with a revealing bra underneath.

Your appearance attracted the wrong kind of attention from co-workers and customers, especially through the snickering and comments about your cleavage. I am certain that you want to be respected for your work rather than your revealing cleavage. It is hard for folks to do both."

"Frannie, your report deadline is on Friday, and I haven't seen a draft yet. Yesterday, I saw you chatting with co-workers on six different occasions. I am concerned that you might not be able to stay on task and have an approved report ready by Friday. I need to have your reassurance that you will have the report at the agreed-upon time."

"Fred, in our meeting this morning, you acted out angrily. You were visibly upset and red in the face, and you spoke loudly and harshly to your co-workers so that they were unwilling to respond to you. I care about you and want you to be successful here, so let's replay that interaction so that your response is more positive the next time."

Notice that all these examples are specific about what happened, when it happened, who was involved, and what the consequences were.

This leaves out the "why." The reason we don't want you to address "why" is because we don't want you to speculate about feelings or motives. Describe observable facts and emotions as they occur. If a person's behavior is unacceptable, the "why" of it doesn't matter. It's unacceptable no matter why it was done. Avoid "why" because questions leading with "why" imply "dummy." Getting such statements clear requires disciplined thought for most of us, so take time to get the issue right before you have your courageous conversation.

Skill #13: Be receptive to coaching from others, and be willing to coach others. Another skill that requires no further explanation.

Skill #14: Resist with a passion the urge to beat around the bush. Most of us have learned that to get along socially, it is best to skirt or avoid sensitive issues, so we don't just go up to each other and say things like, "Gosh, you look awful today. You're only half-shaved, and your shirt looks like you wore it three days in a row." We also don't tell friends or spouses or co-workers when they are embarrassing us with their behavior. We try not to draw attention to mistakes others are making. We usually don't tell people to stop when they are overstepping boundaries. Nor do we tell supervisors we are unhappy because someone else got a raise and we didn't. Instead, we have learned to sidle up to these issues at less stressful moments by referring to them in a joking or otherwise unchallenging way. This avoids a lot of angry confrontations in life, but it also leaves important issues unaddressed and can allow toxic behavior to go unchecked. Sometimes when you're out and about, an unpleasant behavior doesn't matter enough to risk saying anything—but when you're a supervisor in a workplace, you can't let things slide the way you might otherwise. For example, if a man you didn't know made an off-color remark about a woman passing by on the street, you probably wouldn't go out of your way to confront the behavior. However, if you heard a co-worker make a similar remark about a woman in the workplace, you would have to confront the co-worker or risk being accused of contributing to a hostile workplace. When you're having a courageous conversation, sidling up to the issue is just confusing. You need to be direct and clear so there can be no mistake about when, where, what, and who you are talking about. When you beat around the bush, all you get is a beaten-up bush. Other people cannot read your mind, and it is unfair to expect them to. Remember to speak to specific behavior—what people do and say and how they do it and say it. You cannot expect behavior changes from speaking in generalities.

When you're having a courageous conversation, you have already decided to risk conflict (the process of "facing with" others for hopefully a more positive outcome—our definition).

Conflict and Confrontation (a review)

Conflict or confrontation is destructive when it:

- Diverts energy from more important issues, problems, or concerns

- Results in insults, divisiveness, and recurring meanness
- Negatively impacts morale or reinforces poor self-concepts
- Deepens differences in values and biases
- Produces disrespectful and regrettable behavior, such as sabotaging, persistent arguing, name-calling, and prolonged tensions

Conflict or confrontation is constructive when it:

- Clarifies issues of importance
- Results in addressing problems in a helpful way
- Contributes to more positive relationship-building
- Increases receptivity to feedback
- Causes authentic communication to occur
- Reduces the stress of pent-up emotions
- Moves people toward forgiving each other
- Promotes personal growth and confidence-building

Practice Caring Confrontation™ by:

- Arranging for uninterrupted time in a neutral location to talk through issues, problems, or concerns.
- Agreeing on the rules of engagement beforehand. Be sure to engage active listening

techniques, especially where each person takes a turn talking and clarifying what has been heard for accuracy of emotion.

- Setting ground rules for moving forward based on "here's where we are now and here's what we agree to do next." Use words like:

> *"Mindy, I want to _____."*

> *"Moses, here's what is important to me that I want us to _____."*

> *"Martha, what two things do you think we could do together to have less stress in our relationship?"*

> *"Mannix, what are your main goals for us working together? What is the most important thing for me to do for our relationship to be more positive?"*

> *"Muriel, do you sincerely believe that we can have a more positive relationship?"*

> *"Maxwell, would you be willing to forgive me for all that I have done to contribute to the tension between us?"*

Confrontation can be intensely proactive because you describe the problem, clearly stating what you no longer will accept in the relationship based on what is negotiable and what is not. Confrontation provides an emotionally healthier process, allowing you to:

- Face the problem, issue, or concern
- Review and decide on options
- Support others in their options
- Eliminate arguing
- Preempt expected behavior of others

Practice responding with words like:

"Raising your voice does not help. Please stop."

"Name calling or insulting comments like you just made will not help us."

"I wish you could understand my point (where I am on this)."

"Please hear me out as you agreed—without interrupting."

"I will do what I can to help this problem go away."

"I care deeply about where we are—otherwise, I would not be here."

"My heart tells me that you want a better relationship between us."

"Please stop labeling me that way."

*"What we are dealing with does not involve _____.
This issue is between the two of us."*

*"How did you see your going to Fred about me and
this issue as helpful to what we need to do?"*

*"I become frightened when you speak to me in that
tone. I will leave the next time it happens and return
when you are calmer."*

*"My heart tells me that you also care and that you
want less tension in our relationship."*

"What is causing the anger right now?"

"I really care about you, and I am so sorry."

Skill #15: Be responsible and maintain your integrity.
Another thing we learn as children is that it can be easier to
talk with a friend or colleague about what a third party said
about them than it is to tell them our personal opinion. So
we carry that over into work and other adult relationships.
We try to duck hard feelings by not confronting an issue at
all or by blaming the need for the conversation on someone
else. Supervisors do this frequently.

*"I've heard complaints about you taking long lunches.
I don't want to have to be a truant officer."*

*"Tom and Harry told me you are being rude. I don't
want to hear that again."*

"Your report had to be rewritten, but mostly they just changed the words around."

This is an old game called "Let's you and somebody else fight!"

We think supervisors get paid extra because they are supposed to be people of superior vision—hence, "supervisors." They have agreed to be responsible for ensuring that their subordinates are doing well, following policies, and meeting standards. Supposedly they will try to correct behavior as necessary. The best way to do this is with a simple declarative sentence.

"I have learned you are taking longer for lunch than agreed. Today I noticed that your lunchtime went thirty-five minutes over. What kind of problems might your lateness cause? How do you see that as helping teamwork? So here's where we are going from here."

"I have observed you speaking rudely to your co-worker—for example, telling Tommy to 'talk to the hand.' We are going to work together to stop your doing that. My heart tells me that it is not your intention to be rude."

"Your report was unacceptable for the following reasons: _____. It had to be rewritten. Let's take a closer look at how you can prevent those errors in the future."

Get all the relevant information into your issue statement. It needs to be clear that you expect the problem to be addressed, because that's what you get paid to do as a manager and/or supervisor.

Skill #16: Stick to straight talk. Supervisors also try to avoid disappointing their subordinates, often in discussions about promotions and performance appraisals. They'll tell subordinates:

> *"I would have selected you for the promotion if it had just been up to me."*

> *"I wanted to give you an exceptional rating, but my boss has a quota system I couldn't get around."*

What supervisors don't think through is how weak and ineffective these statements make them sound. Besides, subordinates know that supervisors almost always are the deciding officials in these sorts of situations anyway, and what they are really saying is, "I didn't feel strongly enough that you deserved [whatever the good thing was] to fight for you over everyone else." So if you're the supervisor, you may as well say things the way they really are. You'll feel better about the conversation, and so will your subordinates, even though they may not like the message. Again, the best way to approach these conversations is with a simple declarative sentence.

> *"I didn't choose you for the job because _____."*

"I gave you an acceptable rating for the following specific reasons: _____."

Skill #17: Be honest and as caring as possible. It may be that you don't think the employee has enough experience, is nice enough to customers, is quick enough, or is reliable enough; or you may have thought someone else was better suited to fill the organization's needs at that moment. Whatever the reason, that's the thing to say to the employee who wants to know why they weren't chosen, or why they didn't get an outstanding rating.

One caveat: It isn't unusual for organizations in these times to have diversity goals. If that was a factor in your decision, it was perfectly appropriate, but you must be careful how you express it. Discrimination, either favorable or unfavorable, is prohibited. The best way to express the sum of all the factors is to say, "I chose the person I thought would be best for the organization at this time, and I trust you to support that decision and to be welcoming to your new colleague. I know what I am saying is difficult because I have been in the very seat you are now sitting in. However, I found that the longer I held onto the hurt, the more it got in the way. I don't want that to happen to you. I'll do my best to help you and me both through this transition."

The worst thing to say is, "I chose the person because I was told we needed more _____."

Speaking of promotions, it is almost always a mistake to try to tell people exactly what they have to do to get the next promotion. Most selections are competitive among people available when the opportunity occurs. An employee who does everything you said to do to be more promotable still may not be the best person for the job at the next selection.

Be clear about any problems that are keeping employees from being good candidates. If they aren't reliable, if their education isn't up to snuff, if they are missing important experiences, you must tell them. But remember, it's their job to do something about these gaps and to drive their own professional development.

Skill #18: Ask for what you want. Being clear with yourself about what you want to happen as a result of the conversation isn't as easy as you think. If the conversation is about a behavioral issue like getting to work on time or dressing appropriately, the outcome you want can be fairly easy to state. But what if the conversation is about a promotion you did not receive when you thought you should or the fact that your pay has not increased for several years even though you have been doing excellent work? If you already know that you didn't get the promotion, what do you really want out of the conversation? You know your boss isn't going to change the decision already made. If the conversation is about pay, you know that your boss probably can't raise your pay on the spot. So you need to think through what you really want to accomplish with these conversations.

The same things we have already talked about apply. You need to be clear in your own mind about what you want to accomplish with the conversation. Write it down in advance. Practice, practice, practice the conversation with someone whose feedback you value. What you want needs to be reasonably within your or someone else's ability to deliver.

When Subordinates Need to Have Courageous Conversations with Supervisors

Courageous conversations are most frequently thought of as the conversations supervisors and managers have to have with the people who work for them. Oftentimes, though, subordinates are the ones needing to have those conversations with the boss. For example, when employees feel they aren't being treated fairly, are somehow disadvantaged in the workplace, are passed over for promotion, didn't get the work assignment they wanted, or didn't get the appraisal they thought they deserved, they have an issue they need to raise with their boss. These conversations take loads of courage and intensive thought and planning. For example, if your boss gave a promotion you wanted to someone else, it may be upsetting, but you can't reasonably ask the boss to promote you too. You could, however, ask whether you are likely ever to be promoted, what you could do to become more promotable, and whether your boss will support developmental experiences or training for you. How you raise these issues can make a huge difference in the response you receive.

The best way to have a conversation with your boss is to follow the same principles we would tell you to use if you were the boss. Use kind words and remember to look at the situation from the other side. Think your issue through, and state it carefully. Ask for what you want, but be reasonable in your assessment of what is possible under the circumstances. Here are examples of how to raise an issue with your boss:

> *"I am really enjoying my job, and I appreciate the confidence you have shown in me. It has been a point of pride for me that I have been carrying the heaviest workload in our group. When you asked Charlie to take over the _____ assignment, I felt perhaps I wasn't meeting your expectations or that you were losing confidence in me. Is there something I should be doing better than I am?"*

> *"I was really disappointed when I didn't get the assignment to Europe. I know there was a lot of competition for the job even though it wasn't a promotion, and I'm wondering whether there are things I can do to become more competitive." (It's hard for people to understand, but supervisors are reluctant to give up their best subordinates for "plum"*

assignments even though they know the subordinate would like to be selected. It's also one of the areas supervisors are least likely to be honest about.)

"I love my job here and think I'm pretty good at it. I was hoping to be promoted in the last round of promotions, but I wasn't selected. Can we discuss whether I'm doing what I need to be doing to be successful here and whether it's realistic for me to think I will be promoted in the foreseeable future?"

"I was disappointed when I saw that you gave me an 'acceptable' performance appraisal for the past year's work. That seems like a 'C' to me, and I have tried to be an 'A' performer in everything I've ever done. Can you tell me more about what you thought kept me from getting a higher rating and what you think I need to do to excel this year?"

"I don't think you would intentionally exclude part of your workforce from decision-making, but the committee you established doesn't have any women on it. I am concerned that we will send the wrong message to our people if we exclude an entire group from representation." (Note how differently a boss would react to an issue statement like, "You obviously don't care what women think since you didn't put any on your committee.")

It almost never makes any sense for a subordinate to make threats or accusations of unfairness. Your boss can't possibly admit you are right, and you may make the situation much worse than it otherwise would be. For example, if you say to your boss, "You just selected her because you need more women as supervisors," what would you expect your boss's response to be? He or she is not going to say, "Oh gosh, I guess you're right. Wait here while I go cancel the selection." We would advise the boss to respond, "I chose the person I thought would be best for the organization at this time." Similarly, if you say, "Since you don't think I'm worth promoting, I'm going to go out and find another job," how would you expect your boss to react? It isn't rational for you to think he or she is going to say, "Oh no, don't leave. I'll do anything you want." The response we would advise a boss to give would be, "You must do whatever you think is best for your career, but as long as you remain, I will expect you to support my choice for the promotion." We know that sometimes when you are angry or disappointed, you just want to take it out on someone else. That's almost always a terrible mistake, and certainly not emotionally intelligent.

Skill #19: Anticipate what the other person might say. Courageous conversations can't be lectures. The other person has to be part of it too. Once he or she speaks, you never know where things might go. But you can at least think through what the possibilities might be, and how you can respond in a kind and helpful way. Just don't let your preparation dampen your willingness to listen. People are liable to say anything, and you'd better be sure you are listening to what they say, not thinking about what you thought they might say. Once the other person responds, you are faced with a lot of choices. The next few skills offer suggestions.

Skill #20: Try to understand how the other person sees the situation. Sometimes problems can be solved simply by getting each party to see the situation from the other side. It's always worth a try. Here are helpful approaches:

"Tell me how you see this behavior as helpful to you, to our organization."

"Tell me how you see your behavior/appearance/action/attitude/etc. helping you achieve your career/life goals."

"Tell me how you see yourself achieving your goal without doing these things you have not been keeping up with."

"Tell me what you intended to do when others found out about this situation."

"Tell me how you would explain this to the other people counting on you."

"Tell me what you're getting out of this that makes it worth doing."

"Tell me how you see this thing getting done if you don't do it."

"Tell me who you were thinking would pay for this."

"Tell me how you see me trusting you with more responsibility if you continue to do this."

Skill #21: Resist the seductive temptation to argue. No one likes to hear bad news. When you are telling someone they don't measure up in some way, you can't expect them to enjoy hearing it. Expect them to react emotionally. Most people have learned to control their emotions well enough that they don't burst into tears or lash out angrily. But they may defend themselves in other ways, most often by trying to convince you that your opinion is wrong. What happens in the conversation is that they will start asking you questions as a way of getting you to see how wrong you are—and for most of us, the normal reaction to these questions is to defend our position. The whole conversation breaks down into an argument about who's right and who isn't, and both parties end up unhappy, with issues unresolved.

Here's an example of how this might play out in a conversation about a promotion. You say, "I chose another person because I thought they were best for the job at this time." The disappointed employee responds, "What do they have that I don't have? I have more experience here, and I've written more reports." This is where the conversation can quickly fall apart. If you try to argue that the person's experience isn't what it seems to be or that the chosen person is better at one thing or another, you're just going to get into an extended argument. Tell the truth. You chose another person because you thought that individual was better at this time. You appreciate (if you do) the disappointed person's many contributions to your organization. And then the thing to do is to appeal to that person's best nature. Say strongly, "I know I can count on you to support my decision and continue to do your best work."

When people are already disappointed, you can't make them feel better by emphasizing where they fell short. But you do need to let them know that you continue to value them and that you expect them to support your decision. If they want specific coaching on how to become a better candidate, do what you can. If there isn't anything specific they can do, tell the truth.

Sometimes in these conversations, disappointed people will say something rash. They may threaten to seek other employment. Be prepared to address the threat truthfully. If you want them to stay, say so. At the same time, acknowledge that they should do whatever they think would be best for them. If you'd rather they found another job, this would be a good time to say so. If they threaten to undermine or thwart your decision in some way, address the threat directly by telling them you expect them to support your decision. If they can't, you will support them in finding another position. If they threaten to challenge your decision through legal processes, tell them they are welcome to do so—that's why the processes exist. State that you are coming from the point of view that you have done everything in accordance with procedures to the best of your ability. If you can't feel that way about whatever you are doing, then don't do it.

Here are responses that can help you avoid arguments:

"I am not singling you out. If there are other people doing the same thing, I will be having a similar conversation with them. What I want to do right now is address this issue with you."

"The performance standards for someone at your pay level are high, and acceptable performance against those standards is a high achievement. I am not comparing you to other people when I appraise your performance, and I have done my best to give you a thorough and honest assessment."

"I understand you felt provoked. The behavior you engaged in is unacceptable regardless of the provocation. It is part of my job to call that to your attention. My purpose is to help you understand that you cannot be successful in this organization if you continue the behavior."

"The policy you don't like may or may not be inappropriate. We are having this conversation because you deliberately chose not to follow the policy. If you believe the policy should be changed, there are appropriate ways to pursue changes. But while the policy is in place, it is part of my job to be sure it is followed."

People will engage in negative communication styles mainly because they are allowed to get away with it. When people express themselves angrily, or yell, or contradict, or cut others off, or do any of the other things we lump into "negative" communication, it's often because no one has tried to point out to them that they may be causing problems. It's easy enough to do, but most of us learn not to confront unpleasant communication because it often occurs to us in family or school situations where power relationships are exaggerated. For example, it's hard to imagine pointing out to a basketball coach that his open expression of anger may be keeping him from finding important things out. But in a work setting, where information exchange is often crucial to success, it is possible to help people out of negative communication habits by using reasonable sentences to point out how their messages are being received. Here are some examples of sentences you may be able to use to counter negative communication:

"I can see how angry you are. I don't know whether you are angry at me or at someone else, or about

something I don't understand. If you'll give me a chance, I'll try to help you."

"I would never do something on purpose that would be so upsetting for you. There must be a misunderstanding, and I'll fix it if I can."

"Your anger is frightening me, alienating the other people here, and making it impossible for them or me to understand the problem. Let's start with anger management for you."

"Slow down and explain to me what you are so angry about. I can't help you while you're yelling at me." (This is a good one for referees to remember. The most powerful way to respond to the next sentence, which should be an explanation of what the speaker is angry about, is to repeat back to them what they said, demonstrating that you listened to them and understood what they said. Then explain what you did and why, remembering that you may well have been wrong. Sometimes you can correct a mistake, other times you can't. If you can, apologize and do so. Acknowledge your mistake as a matter of integrity.)

"I can't help that I don't understand what you're trying to explain to me. Yelling at me isn't helping me understand. Let's start again at the beginning, and maybe I can explain where I'm not able to follow what you're telling me." (This is a good one

for children whose parents are trying to help them with their homework.)

Skill #22: Enlist the other person's help. One of the most powerful things we can do in a courageous conversation is enlist the other person's help in resolving the situation. Almost all of us are cooperative by nature, and we respond well when there is an appeal for us to help. Remember, no matter how powerful you are, you can't make other people change. They will have to choose to change on their own. It helps if they believe that you are sincerely asking for their help. Here are sentences you can use:

> *"I think you could have a bright future here, and I will support your development. Here's what I desperately need for you to do to help me by improving in this area."*

> *"One of the things I like most about working with you is that I know I can count on your help in situations like this."*

> *"I know my decision doesn't please you, and I am asking for your support."*

> *"I know I can count on you to help us work through this situation."*

> *"You know so much more than I did when I was your age. You'll have to show me how you solve these problems."*

"I love that I have always been able to trust you. I know that I can again on this issue."

"I want you to have the freedom you need. Please help me by checking in occasionally so I'll know things are going okay. Please keep me in the loop."

Skill #23: State your expectations. Courageous conversations have a purpose. You need to know in advance what your purpose is and what kind of outcome you want to achieve. The outcome addresses all the points covered in your issue statement. Be clear about who will do what and by when. State what the other person can trust you to do, and verify that the other person heard you. Ask, "Manny, what exactly did you hear me say that you can trust me to do to address this issue?"

The best way to get the outcome you want is for the other person to be the one proposing the solution. For example, if your purpose is to get the person to dress more appropriately at work, you might ask, "How will you change the way you dress to be less distracting? Less sexually provocative?" If you want to be sure a report will be done on time, you might say, "Tell me exactly (date and time) when I can expect to see a complete first draft of your report." If you need someone to support the person you selected, you might ask, "What will you do to help Bill Hines be successful as a member of this team?"

Other people are more likely to follow through on a solution they propose. You can always negotiate to improve the other person's proposal. Stay focused on the basic principle: the solution needs to be the other person's responsibility.

If the other person can't or won't propose an acceptable solution, be ready with your own. Again, that probably means thinking it through and writing it down before you ever have the conversation. Make sure that you get the person's agreement to support what you propose. Have them identify two or three specifics for support.

Skill #24: Practice persistence and push to the positive. Accept only workable outcomes. Many times you will need to keep bringing the person back to the issue. Remember that many of us are in the habit of avoiding or skirting basic issues. If the person's proposal for solving a situation is "I promise I will try to do better in the future," your response must be, "What specifically will you do differently to solve the problem?" Pin the employee down to specific behaviors. No generalities.

We become skillful and more emotionally intelligent negotiators just by working our way through life in a reasonably successful manner. On the other hand, people are just as skillful at avoiding definite solutions to problems as they are at reaching them. If a person's proposal is, "I promise I will always be at work on time," you need to pin that individual down with exact behavior.

Skill #25: Be truthful. Say, "Here's the truth as I see it," using eleven words or fewer. Address problems and tough, unpleasant issues sooner rather than later. Say, "Here's the tough and unpleasant issue (problem or concern) we need to deal with: _____. And here's the help I need from you."

Allow disagreement. Encourage naysayers and supporters to be heard and acknowledged. Once a decision is made, state your support, and ask for the support of others. A common mistake is believing that you have to agree with someone or something in order to support the person or issue. Maturity in emotional intelligence allows us to successfully support without having to agree. Welcome honesty without retribution. Develop and openly express your expectations around ethical behavior. Create an environment that encourages people to be respectful and sensitive to each other.

Skill #26: Summarize and write the agreement down. This skill also includes letter-writing as a commitment to agreements. Pin down the outcome. Be clear that you are making notes and intend to remember the agreement, and then restate it in its entirety. Get the other person to tell you what they understand the agreement to be. These are serious conversations, or you wouldn't be having them. Careers (including yours) may be substantially affected by what happens as a result of the conversation. Here's how an outcome should sound:

"Here is what I believe we have agreed as a result of our conversation."

"You will do these things: _____."

"I will do these things: _____."

"We will meet again on _____ to review progress. Let's set the date and time now."

It may be advisable or even necessary to state what failure to meet the agreement will lead to. Get the other person to state the consequences. Keep it simple and direct. Make sure the outcome is measurable.

Chapter 3

Examples of Actual Courageous Conversations

*What makes it so difficult to talk straight and address
what needs to be addressed in the clearest way possible?*
—*The Honorable Barbara Jordan*

When exploring opportunities to gain skill in courageous conversations, it may be helpful to study real problems, issues, or concerns that others have shared with us in our training and coaching experiences. The following section contains examples of actual courageous conversations. They are based on real situations that occurred and were successfully addressed in ordinary workplaces. Each of these case studies resulted in positive outcomes for all of the parties involved.

Case 1

Issue statement: "I am aware that since two of your subordinates revealed they are in openly gay relationships, you have refused to speak or assign work to them. The result is the organization has not received the full value for what it pays your subordinates or for your unit as a whole."

Statement of what you want: "I need for you to work effectively with all your subordinates regardless of what your personal feelings about them might be. Tell me what your intentions are for working more effectively with your subordinates."

Conversation: "How do you see refusing to deal with some of your subordinates as being consistent with your responsibilities as a supervisor? Tell me two things you are going to do differently to keep your commitment as their supervisor."

Closing: "I will expect you to assign work, converse, and otherwise treat all your subordinates normally. If you continue to shut some of your subordinates out, I will move to relieve you of your supervisory responsibilities."

Case 2

Issue statement: "You often dress in a way that detracts from your effectiveness. For example, your skirt today is so short that it reveals your underwear. And your choice of tops reveals too much cleavage. I am certain that you want to be remembered for your work, not for showing your underwear and cleavage. Both customers and your co-workers are unable to appreciate the quality of your work because they are distracted by your appearance. I have received three complaints about your appearance already today."

Statement of what you want: "I want you to be successful here because I value what you are capable of doing. I can't allow your dress to continue to detract from your work."

Conversation: "Are you aware that your clothing has affected your credibility here? Tell me three ways you will dress differently so you can highlight your professionalism."

Closing: "I trust you to understand clearly what you need to do. I want to make sure you have a good understanding of what you need to do. Describe two or three ways you will appear more professional at work."

Case 3
Issue statement: "I understand that because of our past hiring practices, we currently have fewer women and minorities in supervisory and managerial positions than we should have if we had been unbiased in our hiring and promotion practices. I agree with our current policy of trying to be fair and increasing our female and minority representation. However, I'm afraid the policy will seriously diminish my own prospects for promotion for the foreseeable future."

Statement of what you want: "Please tell me whether you think I am well-qualified for promotion and whether, in our current climate, I am likely ever to be selected."

Conversation: "What do you see as my strengths, and where do you think I need to improve? Do you think the organization's emphasis on increasing representation means my prospects for promotion in the next two years are bleak?"

Closing: "I will enroll in an online course to improve my statistical analysis skills, and I will count on you to keep me informed about opportunities for advancement."

Case 4

Issue statement: "When I look at the supervisors and managers in our organization, I don't see anyone like me. The main way to achieve higher pay levels here is to become a supervisor, but no one like me has ever been a supervisor. I am concerned that I may not have real prospects for being promoted to a higher level because I am different from the people currently in those jobs."

Statement of what you want: "What is your assessment of my prospects for promotion? What are you willing to do to help me achieve my goals?"

Conversation: "Do you think the organization is likely to continue promoting people who look like the people already in those jobs?"

Closing: "Could I schedule a meeting with you in two weeks so you can share what you learned when you raised this issue with the executive board?"

Case 5

Issue statement: "I have observed that you have a television on while you do your work. I understand you are not disrupting other employees because you use headphones. I do not believe you can work efficiently while you are watching television. I have also received three complaints from customers within the past two months that you have been difficult to deal with and have not fulfilled their requests. In addition, when I asked you to _____ three times in the past two weeks, you brusquely told me you would get to it if you could. Several of your co-workers have mentioned to me that you have been rude to them in the same way."

Statement of what you want: "Stop watching television while you are working, and pay full attention to our customers. You must provide uniformly excellent service to remain in your job. It is also important that we are polite and helpful to each other and to our customers. I can't allow you to continue to treat me, your co-workers, or your customers rudely."

Conversation: "How do you see what you've been doing as helping us serve our customers? Tell me two things you think you can do differently to improve. When you are busy and someone asks you a question, how could you respond so that they don't feel like they've been treated rudely? Let's practice."

Closing: "You won't have a TV on or listen to any device through headphones while you are on duty at your desk. I will arrange for you to be enrolled in our customer-service training as soon as possible. In the meantime, I will assign a person to monitor your conversations for a few days and coach you on how to respond helpfully and politely. I will meet with you in six weeks to give you feedback on how you are doing."

Case 6

Issue statement: "I know you attend AA meetings during your lunch hour. I sensed that your lunch hours have been getting longer, and for the past two weeks I have kept track of how long you've been gone. Three days last week and four days this week, you took more than two hours for lunch. I have noticed you are away from your desk oftentimes for extended periods."

Statement of what you want: "Part of my job is to be sure you are meeting basic work requirements, including being at your workstation, capable of doing good work during your assigned duty hours. I have to insist that you do so."

Conversation: "Walk me through your assessment of this situation right now. How do you see your being away from your work area an average of two hours a day as helpful to your being successful here?"

Closing: "Our organization treats alcoholism as a disease and will make reasonable accommodations for you to rehabilitate, provided you meet the requirements of the program. If you cannot meet your basic work requirements, however, it is my responsibility to take appropriate disciplinary action, which starts with probation and ends with dismissal."

Case 7

Issue statement: "You have been working here as a data-entry clerk for seven years and have done very well. In the past two years, you have applied twice to become a customer-service representative, but each time I selected someone else and counseled you that your communication skills were not at the standard prescribed for the position you are seeking. I value you both as a person and as an employee, and I have decided that, if you want me to, I should try to offer you more specifics about the skills you need to become a customer-service representative. [Assuming permission is granted.] You speak with a heavy regional accent that many people have difficulty understanding. For example, you say 'ax' instead of 'ask,' 'dess' instead of 'desk,' and so on, and you often misspell words on messages and in correspondence. You also get verb tenses and subject-verb agreements wrong, as in 'he had did' and 'she coulda went' and 'they shoulda took care of theyselves.'"

Statement of what you want: "Because I think you could be a good customer-service representative, I want to help you achieve your goals if I can. I would like for you to propose a few practical things you could speak and write so that others can more easily understand you."

Conversation: "Is speaking and writing standard language a skill set you would be willing to improve so that you increase the chances of getting the job you want?"

Close the deal: "If you enroll in the local community college's accent reduction program, standard grammar (English 101-102), I will reimburse you for half the cost. I will also rearrange your hours temporarily so you can attend. I will also give you regular feedback on whether your speech is becoming more understandable."

Chapter 4

Couching Approaches

Sometimes, I just need a little time to get myself ready to talk to folks—just a little time to get my nerve up.
—Geraldine "Cage" Woodley

When we think of the word "couch," several images come to mind. One of these images most likely includes "a comfortable place." Couching language allows you to transition into the courageous conversation from a clear emotional point. If the conversation is difficult, simply say so. For example:

"Serita, this conversation is difficult for me, so please be patient with me."

"Shane, I am very nervous about what I need to say. Please bear with me."

> *"Suzanna, I need a few minutes to get myself together. Please be patient with me."*

Skill #27: If you feel a gap, bridge it. Learn to say, "Evan, here's the gap I am feeling, and here's how I need your help in bridging this gap. Would you please help me?" Or, "Everett, I feel awful that you missed the due date. This rule makes our process as fair as possible, and I am certain that you understand that."

Skill #28: Share information that influenced your feelings and current viewpoints. Say, "Emma, here's how I got to this point." Give two or three concrete examples. State what you want or need.

> *"Ernie, it is past the deadline, and your paperwork has not been filed. You will not be considered in this round of selections."*

> *"Eddie, this is the third time you have missed the deadline. What position do you think that puts me in?"*

Skill #29: State what you are willing to do. Make it clear what your next step would be.

> *"Effie, I'm willing to refer you to my supervisor."*

> *"Elvin, I am willing to sit with you now to review the next round of deadlines."*

"Elisa, here's what I am not willing to do."

Skill #30: Acknowledge the other person's ideas, feelings, thoughts, and facts. Other people need to know they're being listened to, and acknowledging that can steer a conversation in the right direction.

"Isaac, I hear how frustrated you are."

"Irma, let's hear your idea again and see what we can make work."

"Ivan, what's your understanding of the facts? Based on that, let's go over what you need to do."

"Irene, that's the third time you have said you agreed with a statement of mine and then added 'but' and expressed agreement with the opposite."

"Ilsa, Jim, and Harry have done nearly all the talking, and the rest of us have said very little."

Skill #31: Practice corrective commenting. Corrective commenting requires you to provide the exact words that you want to hear others say.

"Jack, please make two complimentary statements about Mary's qualifications. Talk about the last two performance excellence awards she received and her success in leading the process improvement teams."

"Jay, please let me hear you say, 'I will give her idea at least a try.'"

"Jann, here are the exact words I need to hear you say—I know you can say them and that you can follow through." Then you repeat those exact words.

Skill #32: Describe and label for correction. This skill requires you to repeat back to the person exactly what you heard. For example, "Fred, I just heard you say Mary got the job because she's a woman, and we had to meet affirmative-action quotas." Then describe or label the statement: "That's really unfair and darn near sexist. I never saw you that way. Let's talk more about this."

Skill #33: Check on the other person's intentions. This skill gets issues out in the open and allows people to clarify their intentions if they've been misunderstood.

"Jack, is it your intent to sound sexist?" Or, "I'm sure it's not your intent to sound sexist. What exactly did you mean by that statement?"

"Jay, what is the real intent behind what you just said about Mary getting this job?"

"Jeana, I want to be sure of your intent, so would you please repeat what you just said. I want to fully understand where you are."

Skill #34: Make a statement of importance. Oftentimes, stating what is important to you helps others to be aware, to make choices about change, and to actually change their behavior.

> *"Lennie, it is really important to me that you are helpful on this project, and here are the specific behaviors I look at as helpful."*

> *"Lucy, let me describe how important your presence is here."*

> *"Lindsey, tell me how important you think your delivering on these tasks is to me."*

Skill #35: Strongly state "please" with "stop." This simple yet powerful skill makes it clear to others that you are asking them to stop saying things and doing things not helpful to positive relationship building.

> *"Oscar, please stop making what feels like sarcastic statements as your colleagues are presenting their suggestions."*

> *"Onie, please stop coming to work, clocking in, and then going to have breakfast for an hour before you actually start working."*

> *"Ollie, please stop asking me for money."*

Skill #36: Say no without guilt. Many people with whom we work tell us that they feel guilty when they say no. But you're not doing your co-workers any favors by beating around the bush. Say no politely but firmly:

> *"Zane, I have to say no to your request. Right now, I am tapped out."*

> *"Zerita, my answer is no, and I need you to respect that."*

> *"Zachary, 'no' is still the answer, and here are the reasons."*

Skill #37: Put the accent on one-word reactions. When someone makes a negative, nasty, mean, hateful, or totally inappropriate comment, look him or her squarely in the eye and say with emphasis:

> *"Pardon?"*

> *"Really?"*

> *"What?"*

Ask the person to repeat the statement. You respond by asking for the behavior you want.

Skill #38: Draw the relationship comparison. Sometimes, using personal relationships as a reference can help people see an error in their thinking. For example,

"Van, I just heard you make a comment about how certain jobs are not for women. How would you like it if someone said that about your daughter, Megan? How would you like it if they deliberately kept her out of a job she really wanted and that she was good at?"

Skill #39: Implement peer modeling. This powerful technique allows a person of the same peer group (gender, rank, group, ethnicity, etc.) to offer correction or assistance by pointing out a behavior in the hope that feedback from the peer-group member may be better received. "Pete, as one supervisor to another, I would hate to see a grievance filed against you for what you just said. How about checking your thinking before making those kind of statements?"

Skill #40: Show a sense of humor. You can often defuse charged situations by making a joke instead of taking offense.

> *"Sam, I'll agree not to call you poopsie if you agree to stop calling me sweetie."*

> *"Sherri, let's have a good laugh about this potential misunderstanding and call it a day."*

> *"Sara, one of my shortcomings, among many, is opening my mouth to exchange feet! Please forgive me and give me a fresh start."*

Skill #41: Ask clarifying questions. Use this skill when an uncomfortable gesture or statement has been clearly misunderstood.

> *"Jake, I have asked you at least three times to stop making sexually explicit comments to me. Why have you ignored me?"*

> *"Jake, what am I doing that makes you think I'm interested in you in a sexual way?"*

> *"Jake, I sense by your behavior that you want a sexual harassment charge filed against you. Is that right?"*

Chapter 5

Practical Applications

*Just take a little more time to think through
the outcomes you want and keep trying.
Why do we make talking so hard?*
—*Dr. Violet Henighan*

This chapter describes specific tools we have developed over several years. When shared with participants and clients in relationship to specific areas of concern and put into practice, these skills provide options for several courageous conversations.

Skill #42: Revisit an old or lingering issue through "the polite return." Have you ever thought of exactly what you wanted to say in response to a situation requiring courage, yet you did not return to the person? You kept thinking about it and wishing you had said what you thought of later. This skill allows you to return to an individual and revisit a previous situation.

> *"Jerry, I've had a chance to reflect on our exchange last month about _____. [Describe the exchange as vividly as you can remember.] I could not think of what I wanted to say. I'd like to revisit that issue now."*

> *"Janey, I want to revisit the confusion we had last week about the change in the schedule."*

> *"Jarrett, let's go together to Max, revisit the team issues, and offer our suggestions."*

There is no statute of limitations on polite returns to revisit an issue, problem, or concern. This skill is helpful in surfacing and addressing old or recurring issues and lingering resentments.

Skill #43: Say a "preemptive thank-you" for the behavior you want. This skill allows you to thank an individual for doing or saying the right thing before it is actually done.

> *"Kerry, thank you, in advance, for speaking positively about Mary's qualifications. I felt certain I could count on you to do the right thing."*

"Kenna, thank you for saying 'thank you.' It means a lot to me to hear that."

"Kathy, I know you will thank me for bringing this issue to you."

Skill #44: Use humility to prompt awareness of behavior. What we call "the humble assertion" prompts others to think about the impact of what they are saying.

"Lenny, I just heard you say that Mary got the job because she's a woman. Think about that for a minute. What did Mary do to deserve such an insensitive comment?"

"Lorna, I've always seen you as a humble and caring person. Mary's the same way. Let's give her a chance."

"Lacey, what can we do to make Mary feel more welcome? Let's work together on that."

Skill #45: Confront with caring. This skill allows you to challenge the other person to a more appropriate response.

"Marvin, would you be willing to say what you just said about Mary in front of our manager and especially in front of Mary?"

"Mavis, what you just said about Mary sounds so mean. How is it helpful in making her to feel welcome?"

"Myrna, I want to challenge what you just said. How did you reach that conclusion?"

Skill #46: State how you feel and what you found. Use this empathy skill when you have legitimately experienced the same situation as the person with whom you are talking. For example, "Nina, I hear your disappointment that you did not get the job. Believe me, I know it feels worse than awful because I have been right where you are, emotionally torn-up. So I know how rotten you feel, because I have felt what you are feeling right now. Yet I found that continuing to stay in this wretched funk got in the way of my ability to regroup and move forward. I don't want to see that happen to you. Here's what I am willing to do to help you move forward."

Skill #47: Name body language. Don't let people get away with wordless gestures.

"Petra, what's with the eye-rolling? What were you thinking that prompted that reaction?"

"Polly, I see your arms crossed and your jaw clenching. Please share your feelings so we can be sure of where you are and what we need to do next."

"Peterson, I heard you sighing just now when the change was announced. Go over with us what prompted the sighing. Let's talk through that."

Skill #48: Present real data to support your position. Use numbers—specific quantitative information—to position dialogue.

"Quinn, this is the third time this week you have been more than fifteen minutes late for work."

"Quanita, how do you see your handing in the last three reports late as helping you to get a superior performance rating?"

"Quincy, that is the second time this month I've noticed you complimenting Craig and Doris on their teamwork. That is just wonderful!"

Skill #49: State a clear compromise. Set the stage for workable compromise with a "when/then" sentence.

"Rex, when you demonstrate your willingness to be at your desk and working promptly at 8:30 for six consecutive weeks, then we can consider other assignments for you."

"Regina, when you overcome your tendency to procrastinate, which produces late reports, then we can talk about a possible promotion."

> *"Randolph, when three months go by without a single customer complaint on you, then we can talk about the next level."*

Remember that compromises only have to work—they don't necessarily have to be fair.

Skill #50: Obey the two-to-one rule. When approaching someone who is especially resistant, position your responses to have twice the positive outcome for the resister. What are the benefits to the other person?

> *"Sanford, here are two direct benefits that I know you will agree with."* Describe those benefits clearly for the resistant person.

> *"Shanita, how will it hurt you to keep your agreements?"*

> *"Samuel, let's agree on at least two benefits for getting this done."*

Skill #51: State strongly what you will do. Use the term "for you" to increase the other person's willingness to listen.

> *"Talley, I can be an even more effective subordinate for you when you delegate the assignment to me and give me a date to review it with you."*

"Thelma, I know now, since the training program, what a pain in the neck I have been for you. Please forgive me, and thank you for not giving up on me."

"Toma, for you, I welcome the opportunity to work overtime, especially the way you respect each of us on the team."

Skill #52: Be generous with compliments. When communicating with individuals, use "the complimentary lead" to open the conversation with sincere appreciation.

"Uma, I love it when you delegate this kind of project to me and trust me to get it done."

"Ulice, you sounded strong and on point during your presentation."

"Ulysses, you have got too much going for you to let your appearance detract from your credibility."

Skill #53: Acknowledge the power of others with a "deferential pass." Used effectively, this skill allows you to pass the power to individuals who are in a position to assist you.

"Verle, you have the power to say yes to this request."

"Virginia, you have the power to help the tension in this office go away."

"Vickie, you have the power to contribute to the healing we so desperately need."

Skill #54: Recognize and utilize the power of forgiveness.
Use the actual word *forgive* to bridge relationships.

"Winston, please forgive me for not having spoken to you sooner about your tardiness. I really should have. Here's where we're going from here."

"Will, please forgive me for what I did to contribute to the confusion. Can we start over?"

"Winifred, please know that I forgive you for that remark you just made about people from my state. I know you did not mean to be insulting."

Skill #55: Be pliant or bend toward the style of others.
Make a focused effort to express more appreciation and flexibility toward persons whose styles are decidedly different from yours. This skill helps you to increase your patience, learn to go with resistance, not take things so personally, and value diversity. For example, to address micromanaging: "It's okay with me if you keep checking on me on the assignment. Some people might call it micromanaging. I know how concerned you are about the work, so it is okay with me." Agree when someone criticizes you; for example, if a co-worker says, "That outfit really looks too small for you," respond with, "You're right, it is too small." Practice going with the person's style instead of fighting it.

Chapter 6

Picking Your Battles

Sometimes there is as much risk in saying nothing as in saying something.
—*Elsie Hines*

Communicating toward better outcomes remains a lifelong goal for most of us. It really is a journey that requires diligent awareness, patience, continual learning, and tireless effort. Some battles are simply not worth picking. Perceived slights can be overlooked. Sometimes other folks may be seen as entertainment or through more forgiving eyes.

Skill #56: Don't bite! Not every issue warrants a confrontation. Some battles are simply not worth picking. Be attentive to listening for the difference between descriptive criticism and personal-growth criticism. Watch your tendency to bite unnecessarily. Remember to repeat frequently, "Don't bite—don't bite—don't bite!" Remember that people cannot get your goat if they don't know where it is hidden.

Skill #57: Practice positive persistence. Simply don't give up. Remind people that you will return to "revisit" issues.

> *"Priscilla, I have had several days to think about what you said, and I want to revisit the issue about _____."*

> *"Xavier, last week when you commented that I was pigheaded, I was stunned and did not know what to say. Please help me revisit that issue, because I certainly don't want to be seen that way."*

Skill #58: Say please and thank you. Ask for help, receive help, and be generous in helping others.

> *"Yancy, please help us with this project by agreeing to do the following."*

> *"Yogi, thank you for offering to help with this tense situation. Your offer to help says that you really care about this team."*

"Yolanda, here's where I am struggling, and here's the help I need."

Skill #59: Set the scene strategically. This skill requires you to pay close attention to timing, location, and the immediate area where a courageous conversation takes place. These are all the elements of appropriate scene-setting.

"Zerita, please let me treat you to a cup of tea and run something by you that I need your guidance on." Open the conversation with, "Here's what I am struggling with."

"Zachary, could we please go to a more quiet place with no phone interruptions? I desperately need your undivided attention."

"Zoe, tomorrow morning at 11:00 would be a good time. That way, you will be done with the staff meeting. I will stop by and pick you up for an early lunch."

Skill #60: Make a peace offering. This skill allows you to open the door to communication by presenting an actual peace offering—card, flowers, special gift, etc. The peace offering goes beyond the minimum expectation of "thank you" or "I'm sorry."

"Alisa, please accept this roll of Life Savers for reminding me of my pigheadedness. Please forgive

me—I will continue to work on my patience and listening. You really are a life saver for me."

"Artie, here's a bouquet as a gesture of my surrender on the proposal. You are right about what we need to do."

"Anderson, I am treating the entire staff to Dove bars as my peace offering for being such a jerk in the staff meeting yesterday."

Skill #61: Be an ego-enhancer. By consciously focusing on the ego of others, we can be more positive when placing our words.

"Burt, I love that you are taking the time to help me with my pigheadedness. You're the best."

"Barry, you have the ability to help lead us through this tension. Where do we need to start?"

"Benita, your peaceful spirit adds so much to our teamwork."

Skill #62: State your outcome. With this skill, your focus is on expected outcomes with agreement to identify specific next steps.

"Conan, here are the two main outcomes I expect of you from this conversation."

"Cory, what do you see as the next two or three expected outcomes from this conversation we are having now?"

"Constance, right now the most immediate next step for you as the team leader is to _____."

Skill #63: Write relationship-positive letters or notes. This skill returns you to the traditional skill of writing letters and notes, and selecting cards with the goal of improving relationships.

Dear Boss,

Thank you for the opportunity to attend the training on _____. While I was there, I learned several skills that will help me to be an even more effective subordinate for you. I look forward to meeting with you to share at least five of those skills with you as soon as I return.

Again, I thank you!

Skill #64: Paint a descriptive picture. This skill requires you to describe in clear detail how something looks, smells, sounds, and feels. Using vivid details allows you to paint pictures of situations and their potential impact.

"Dusty, let me describe how this _____ looks to me."

"Devon, how does this tension feel to you and the rest of the team?"

"Daisy, what you just said about Freda sounds a little squiggly to me. Let me get her right now so that we can clear this situation up immediately."

Skill #65: Make trust statements. Actually use the word *trust* when communicating with others.

"Edwina, I completely trust you to keep your word."

"Edita, what would it take for us to start rebuilding a more trusting relationship?"

"Essie, here's what I need to trust you to do."

Skill #66: Lead with care. Let the people you work with know that you care about them and the work they do.

"Fila, I really care about you and I want _____"

"Foster, here's what I really care about."

"Fannie, I heard you say you care about our team's success. Two of your assignments have not been turned in. How does that square with your saying you care about our team's success?"

Skill #67: Ask for success. This skill helps you to ask for exactly what you want.

> *"Geri, would you help us be successful with _____?" (Ask for what you want.)*

> *"Gentry, how do you see your _____ as helping you to be successful here?" (Describe specific behavior.)*

> *"Grover, how do you see your behavior helping our relationship to be successful?" (Describe specific behavior.)*

Chapter 7

Summary

"Every single one of us can work harder at communicating better. It is truly a life-long pursuit."
—*Geraldine Woodley*

Talking straight in caring and thoughtful tones; recording our emotions, reactions, and wishes; and reaching out to people in our lives all combine to help us move more effectively through differences. As humans, we are all broken in some way and need each other to get better. We grew into the people we are through our relationships with others. Therefore, we can grow into who we can become through more attentiveness to our relationships with others.

Skill #68: Use the straight-talk skills you've learned.
Constantly review the skills that help promote relationship building:

- Project positive expectations.

    "I will have an answer to you by _____."

    "I will be glad to _____."

    "This is what I'm willing to do: _____."

    "I will be happy to support you on _____."

    "I want to _____."

    "I can _____."

    "Thank you for _____."

    Practice the art of "gracious outs" that allow people to save face. This skill also includes the art of the apology by acknowledging the wrong or potential wrong, hurt, or insult; stating your intentions for making amends; asking for trust in your future behaviors; sharing the insights you have gained; and expressing faith in the future of your relationship.
- Refuse to be a victim, helpless, or powerless.
- Deliver at least three compliments a day.
- Ask for what you want in specific language.
- Make being pleasant, caring, and helpful a priority in all of your relationships.

- Be attentive to opportunities to build and rebuild relationships.
- Eliminate clutter in your personal space and relationships.
- Accept responsibility for your half of every relationship you have.
- Practice, practice, practice emotional intelligence and positive communications.
- Practice good listening habits.
- Welcome change in your behavior, and help others in changing their behaviors.
- Promise only what you can deliver; keep your word.
- Develop good delegating practices.
- Be flexible in embracing the styles of others.
- Trust your team members.
- Develop and maintain cooperation.

Skill #69: Understand the management of differences.
Apply emotional intelligence in the management of differences. Mark L. Rosen writes, "We admire traits in others that we admire in ourselves; we denigrate others when their behavior doesn't conform to our values. We find it almost impossible to climb inside someone else's head and see the world through different eyes." When differences occur, remember that strong feelings are frequently aroused, objectivity diminishes, and egos are threatened. Personal relationships may be jeopardized, especially when people

have been taught different beliefs about what constitutes appropriate behavior, and believe that "different" means "wrong." The ability to deal with conflict depends upon:

- Willingness to diagnose and understand differences
- Awareness of and choice to select appropriately from a variety of behaviors
- Flexibility to promote resolution

Accept these basic assumptions that:

- Differences among people are not inherently "good" or "bad"
- There is no single "right" way to deal with differences
- Problems cannot be solved with the same thinking that got you into the problems

What is the nature of the differences?

- Differences over beliefs
- Differences over facts
- Differences over goals
- Differences over procedures
- Differences over values

What phase am I in when addressing differences?

- Anticipation
- Conscious but unexpressed difference
- Conscious but unexpressed indifference

- Open to discussion
- Open conflict—win, lose, or compromise
- Forgiveness

Select an approach to differences and own your choices. Ask yourself:

- What actions are available to me? What am I willing to do to help move beyond this point of impasse?
- What must I keep in mind in selecting the best course of action from among the available alternatives?
- When is the approach appropriate?

How do you deal with differences?

- Differences may be avoided
- Differences may be repressed
- Differences can be sharpened into conflict
- Differences can be utilized in problem-solving that helps relationships

The major difference between an emotionally healthy relationship and one that may be toxic is the depth of "freedom feeling" to express yourself without fear of reprisal.

When transforming emotional conflict, consider the question: What can I do to transform emotional conflict into more positive outcomes?

- Welcome the existence of differences. "Let's explore the differences we have over _____."
- Listen with understanding rather than evaluation. "I want to make sure I am listening for understanding."
- Clarify the nature of the conflict. "Here's my understanding of the nature of this conflict."
- Recognize and accept the feelings of the individuals involved. "Here's what I am feeling right now."
- Clarify the next steps. "Where do you suggest we go from here?"
- Give primary attention to maintaining relationships. "It is so important to me that we maintain a good relationship between us."
- Express thanks for willingness to help you. "Thank you for helping me work through this issue."

Skill #70: Journal to managing conflict. Describe a current issue, problem, or concern in which you are not satisfied, and about which you would like to be more positive. In selecting a situation, consider the emotional consequences of leaving it the way it is now. Use the following guidelines in making your selection.

- It is important to you (your team, your family, your organization, etc.)
- It involves interaction between you and at least one other person

- It is a situation that you are willing to address through courage
- It is not yet solved but is potentially solvable
- It is a problem that others can help you with

What is your position, role, or relation to this problem—how are you involved? (Answer in ten words or less—"focused framing" keeps you from whining.)

_____

_____

_____

_____

What are the two main causes of the problem, and why does it continue to exist? (Ten words for each of the causes)

_____

_____

_____

_____

Describe your own feelings and emotions about the problem, the key person involved, and any special challenges you have.

_____

_____

_____

_____

Who else is affected by the problem? In what way?

_____

_____

_____

_____

What is the impact of the problem on you?

_____

_____

_____

_____

What is likely to happen if you choose not to address this issue? (Ten words or less)

_____

_____

_____

_____

What have you personally tried to do in the recent past about this problem? (List specific actions.)

_____

_____

_____

_____

List two other possible actions that you could take.

_____

_____

_____

_____

What would you do if you felt more confident? If you were really not afraid?

_____

_____

_____

_____

In ten words or less, frame your opening response to addressing your situation.

_____

_____

_____

_____

When emotional differences occur, strong feelings are frequently aroused, objectivity diminishes, egos become threatened, power plays occur, and personal relationships may be jeopardized. Emotional intelligence to deal with conflict depends on your ability to assess and understand differences, and your awareness of and skill in selecting appropriately from a variety of words to address issues.

When selecting an approach to addressing emotional differences, ask yourself:

- What actions are available to me?
- What must I keep in mind in selecting the best course of action from among the available alternatives?
- When is the approach appropriate?

Remember, differences can be avoided. Differences may be repressed. Differences can be applied for problem-solving. Ask, "How can we build on our differences?"

Skill #71: Listen, listen, listen. Here are ten steps for minimizing conflict.

1. Stop talking. Remember that you have two ears and one mouth. Spend twice as much time listening as you do talking.
2. Empathize with others. People are rational from their point of view. Ask questions for clarity and understanding. Remember to avoid *why*. Practice patience.
3. Concentrate on really hearing the other person.
4. Show the other person that you want to listen, and express this wish openly.
5. Put others at ease. "Let's sit together and take a closer look at this issue."

6. Be aware of and name your emotions and your biases. "Here's where I am emotionally, and here's the bias I am struggling with."

7. Control your emotions, especially anger. Take a twenty-minute break.

8. Control distractions—phones, clutter, drop-in visitors, tight calendar.

9. Stay on the main points and state them. "Here are my main two points."

10. Acknowledge the emotions of others.

Skill #72: Keep learning and practicing emotional-intelligence skills. Useful books to study and apply:

Brown, Elizabeth. *Living Successfully with Screwed Up People*. Grand Rapids, MI: Fleming H. Revel Press, 2008.

Bradberry, Travis, and Greaves, Jean. *Emotional Intelligence 2.0*. San Diego, CA: TalentSmart Press, 2009.

Goleman, Daniel. *Social Intelligence*. New York: Bantam Dell, 2007.

Goleman, Daniel. *Working with Emotional Intelligence*. New York: Bantam Dell, 2006.

Patterson, Kerry, et al., *Crucial Conversations*. New York: McGraw-Hill, 2002.

Rath, Rom and Clifton Donald O., *How Full Is Your Bucket*. New York: Gallap Press, 2005.

Ruiz, Miguel, *The Four Agreements*. San Rafael, CA, 1997.

Sutton, Robert I., *The No Asshole Rule: Building a Civilized Workplace and Surviving One That Isn't*. New York: Business Press, 2007.

About the Authors

For more than twenty years, Dr. Carolyn C.W. Hines served as president and co-owner of C&W Associates, Inc., a human resources development corporation with 310 employees. Currently, she is president of C.W. Hines and Associates, Inc., specializing in dispute resolution, executive coaching, workforce diversity, management consulting and training, emotional-intelligence skill building, organizational development, collaborative technology-based strategic planning, team building, and transformational leadership.

Carolyn received her undergraduate education at Saint Paul's College in Lawrenceville, Virginia, and at Wellesley College, Wellesley, Massachusetts. She holds three graduate degrees, including a doctorate in counseling and higher-education administration from the College of William and Mary in Williamsburg, Virginia.

Carolyn is a licensed professional counselor, marriage and family therapist, and certified relationship specialist, and she has been certified as a mediator by the Virginia Supreme Court and a mediator and arbitrator by the National Association of Securities Dealers. She holds Diplomate and LIFE Status in the American Psychotherapy Association. She is certified as an executive coach by the National Center for Healthcare Leadership, The National Coaching Academy, Envisia 360 (Relationship Intelligence), and the Strength Deployment Institute

William A. Hines Jr., executive vice president and co-owner of C.W. Hines and Associates, Inc., an international management training and consulting firm based in White Stone, Virginia, completed his undergraduate education at Hampton University, where he received a bachelor of science degree in business management. He was awarded a master's degree in human resources management from George Washington University. He is also a graduate of the Peninsula Chamber of Commerce/Christopher Newport University Leadership Institute and the Armed Forces Staff College in Norfolk, Virginia, and the Command and General Staff College.

A decorated Vietnam veteran (Bronze Star and Legion of Merit) and a retired lieutenant colonel, his outstanding military career included several successful command assignments in Europe and Vietnam. His final Pentagon assignment was as inspector general, where he received commendations for outstanding work conducting focus groups throughout the United States, Europe, and Korea. Bill holds certification in nonviolent conflict resolution from the Martin Luther King Center in Atlanta, Georgia, and he is a certified relationship specialist and mediator (the Virginia Supreme Court).

LaVergne, TN USA
19 September 2010
197642LV00001B/53/P